FURNITURE DOCTORING
and
FRENCH POLISHING

FURNITURE DOCTORING

and

FRENCH POLISHING

by

CHARLES HARDING

LONDON

W. FOULSHAM & CO. LTD.

NEW YORK . TORONTO . CAPE TOWN . SYDNEY

W. FOULSHAM & CO. LTD.,
Yeovil Road, Slough, Bucks., England.

572-00710-8

Made & Printed in Great Britain by
John Gardner (Printers) Ltd.
Liverpool 20

CONTENTS

INTRODUCTION

There has been a tremendous upsurge in interest in antique furniture over the last decade or two, and far more people search for, and often find, antique pieces within the limits of their pockets.

The field is wider and the opportunities greater, for us than for previous generations, now that Victoriana has come within the classification of *antique*. This is not because the Victorians had more furniture, but because they were, as a generation, characterised by a tendency to cherish their possessions to an extent that almost amounted to parsimony. This was the age of the doily, the runner and the little tablecloth to protect furniture surfaces; of the antimacassar to keep upholstery clean; of the proud display of fine china in glass-fronted cabinets; of the cheap domestic servant with the strong arm, and the soft linen cloth; of the unemancipated daughter of the house whose chores included the care of such ornaments, pictures and fine furniture that could not be left to domestic hands.

While we deplore the Victorian way of life, we reap the benefit of their possessive care in a heritage of very well preserved furniture, much of it fetching a very high price. Almost all of us would like to be able to buy such furniture at Southerby's or Christies at top prices, but most of us have to search a bit to find pieces at more accommodating prices, and the actual search for such pieces is part of the fun of collecting.

Of course, in spite of the care our Victorian forbears lavished on their furniture, a great deal of it suffered enough wear and tear to reduce its value considerably. Few people give thought to the future antique value of their furniture while it is actually in use in their home. In ten years, furniture becomes boring, in twenty it is unfashionable, in forty years a joke. Thirty years ago, one could buy a Victorian lady chair for a few shillings, often with its original, though tatty, upholstery; a washstand with its original milk paint surface (under a great number of soft paint layers) might go for perhaps 2/6. Huge heavy veneer-top dining tables could be had for virtually nothing, and wardrobes could be, and still are, bought as cheap timber and land up as rabbit hutches or dog kennels.

The restoration of antique furniture is not difficult (as this book will show you), but it is time-consuming. The owner of an antique shop usually has a long think before he decides to embark on a lengthy restoration job, because it is often the man-hours taken to restore a piece that puts its price up. He may well decide that its not worth *his* while to put the time in. He may not even have the time available, because there is more furniture around needing restoration than there are restorers to deal with it. This is why good pieces with superficial damage find their way onto the general market, often at a very reasonable price, and if you have seen such pieces, and wondered if it is possible for the ordinary do-it-yourself enthusiast to tackle the job with a reasonable chance of success on a professional level, the answer is—yes, you can.

That is what this book is all about. It is a short commonsense guide to the professional way in which surfaces can be dealt with. It shows that furniture refinishing is not only possible, but downright easy if tackled properly, and if you are prepared to take a reasonable amount of time about it.

Everything in this book applies, of course, to surface damage in modern furniture, and in considering the correct maintenance of much of the extremely good pieces, especially teak and oak pieces and the excellent modern arm-chairs, it is a good thing to remember that in another hundred years, the best of these will fetch a high price in the antique market. If they survive the changing fashions, and remain in the hands of your heirs and assigns, they will form as good, or even a better legacy than actual cash in these days of depreciating money values.

But not everything that reaches the age of a hundred years accrues in value. You have to start with the best that can be obtained at any particular moment. Every age produces its junk. The Victorians produced a tremendous amount of it.

It fetches a high price today for its *amusement* value. It might be a good idea to remember that a hundred years hence, the public sense of humour may have changed, and our present day junk may simply be considered junk, and dealt with accordingly.

CHAPTER 1

Furniture First Aid

White Spots and Rings

The saddest thing that ever happened to furniture surfaces was the passing out of fashion of little table cloths and doilys. The immediate reaction to them today is that they are fussy, fuddy-duddy and ridiculous, but the price we pay for their passing is that our furniture surfaces have become more vulnerable, just when fashion decrees their importance.

The degree of this vulnerability varies in direct ratio to the quality of the furniture finish. Not always, unfortunately, with its cost. Often high-priced factory furniture is finished with a poor-grade lacquer, which actually blenches at a touch of water or a hot plate. The resulting white ring or spot remains on the surface for all time, unless we do something to remove it.

Cheap lacquers are the only surfaces that mark in this way. A good-grade of lacquer will not white-spot, neither will a sealer-finish, nor a varnish finish.

Very well, a white spot on your table-top is a black mark against the furniture manufacturer, or, if the piece is antique, against the restorer, known or un-known, who applied a cheap lacquer finish during restoration. Lacquer wasn't invented until the 1900's, and was soon divided into a number of grades of quality, and cheap-jack restorers have had a field-day ever since.

Actually, white spot trouble is easy to cure, because this is only surface damage. Simply rub the spots with cigar ash wetted to a paste with a few drops of water.

If you are (a) a non-smoker, (b) a non-cigar smoker, or if this method doesn't work (there is an occasional modern finish that doesn't respond), dampen a small pad of cotton cloth with ammonia and whisk it gently over the surface. Don't rub. It's the fumes that are doing the work. Or use cellulose thinner in exactly the same manner.

Applying a Waterproof Finish

Of course, you may find life a trifle irritating with a table that shows every water or heat-mark, and you may decide that you would prefer to treat the whole surface of your table to make it resistant to water and even to alcohol. This is particularly advisable if the lacquer is of such poor standard that these stains penetrate below the surface, in which case you are going to have to rub with grade 000 or 0000 steel wool, not just over the white mark but over the whole surface, to achieve an even sheen. Once you have done this, you will be certain that there is a better way. There is, and the better way is to varnish the whole surface.

A great many people approach the idea of varnishing with trepidation, because they have been plagued in the past with bubbles and specks of dust that mar the surface, however carefully applied. But further on in this book, we set out the cardinal rules for perfect varnishing—perfect enough to stand the scrutiny of your friends and your enemies, who are out to criticise your furniture surfaces.

And it's quite easy, too, if you follow our instructions.

Heat marks are another very common spoiler of furniture surfaces, and again, a really good lacquer finish will stand up to a certain amount of heat without marking, while a cheaper finish will show heat marks very easily.

Actually, in a great number of cases, a heat mark is primarily a water stain, and shows itself as a white spot or ring. This is because atmosphere, even in these days of central heating, is always moist to a certain degree, and the putting of, say, a hot plate onto a dining room table causes a small layer of steam to collect. This can be treated in the same ways as for white spots and rings, as explained in the previous section.

Where heat has damaged the actual finish of your piece of furniture, you can try one of the following methods:

(a) For lacquer or varnish finishes, rub vigorously with a little silver polish on a soft cloth.

(b) Or pour no more than two drops of methylated spirits on a pad of cotton wool, cover the pad with a couple of thicknesses of muslin, and rub over and around the mark. If you're lucky, you will shift sufficient finish from the surrounding area to cover the burned part, but of course, this only works for comparatively small burns. If you've really vandalized your furniture, you're going to have to use re-amalgamation, (see page 22,) a job of some magnitude which should teach you to be more careful in future.

If your furniture is wax polished, melt a little good quality wax polish, and carefully pour just enough to replace the missing polish. When quite dry and hard, scrape with infinitesimal care, and a blunt blade, such as the *back* of a table knife, until the whole surface is level. Then polish like mad with a soft cloth, and go on polishing until the gloss is restored.

Of course, these methods only apply to relatively superficial heat damage. If you've destroyed the actual wood, you're in real trouble. When the spot is small, treat as for cigarette burns (see following section,) but if the area is deep and wide, if, for instance, someone has left a hot iron on the surface, take a bit of thought about the value of the piece and how much you love it before you proceed any further. Because if the area is too big for a spot of surface-faking, such as Beaumontage (chapter 3), you are going to have to strip and sandpaper the whole surface, and restain and refinish it. It may be better to get an expert to do it for you!

If your piece has a veneer surface, the same chapter will tell you how to replace missing pieces, but results can't be guaranteed if the area is too large.

A friend of mine, a rather half-hearted do-it-yourselfer, says that if you are faced with a very large, very deep burn which destroys the actual wood, there is only one thing to do with it. Complete the job, he says, and burn the whole thing. And buy yourself an ample number of heat-proof table mats before you buy another table.

Cigarette Burns

What cigarette burns do to a furniture surface shouldn't happen to a dog. In fact, if it happened to a dog, the R.S.P.C.A. would have something to say about it. But there is no protection society for tables. Short of making cigarette burns a capital crime, they must be regarded as inevitable, and dealt with in the best possible way.

Dealing with cigarette burns is not particularly easy, but professional help tends to be expensive (at least £2 a burn), and the method we set out here will probably be as satisfactory as anything a professional can achieve.

There are two alternative methods:

METHOD ONE

(a) Scrape the burned area smooth with a curved blade, such as a jack-knife blade, and then smooth with a very small piece of sandpaper.

(b) Get some artist's oil colours, and use them straight from the tube, undiluted, mixing them until you have an exact colour-match with the surrounding area.

(c) Smudge the colour into the scraped area *as thinly* as possible, so that it will dry hard, until it matches the surrounding area.

(d) When quite dry, spray with one coat of clear plastic.

(e) When quite dry, spray the whole surface again with clear plastic, to get an even refraction when viewed from any angle.

(f) Rub the whole surface with fine steel wool, and wax according to instructions given on page 57.

METHOD TWO

This is a better method if the burn has gone deeply into the wood. After scraping the burned area, fill the depression with suitably coloured beeswax, and treat it as for chipped veneer, dealt with in the next chapter.

Worn Spots and Edges

Simple wear, in which the finish has become dulled, while the wood and stain remain intact, can be easily corrected by applying Overcoating, which is explained on page 21.

Deep wear, in which the area of wear is lighter in colour than the rest of the surface, needs a little more work.

DEEP WEAR

Start at the edges, and restore colour with iodine, or black or brown ink, using the side of a water-colour brush. Or, if none of these seem a very good colour match, mix water colours to an exact match. When the colour has completely dried, spray or brush over with shellac to prevent rubbing-off.

A deep-wear area in the centre of a surface, such as a table, is not quite so easy to deal with, and may take a little more patience. Since the centre area is more eye-catching, (and subject to continued wear), it is better to buy artist's oil paints, and work to get an exact match, wiping off unsatisfactory colours with a rag moistened with turpentine.

Here's how it's done:—

(a) Apply the mixed oil paint with a pad, not a brush, in a process known as 'wiping-on', smudging the paint at the edges so that no join is visible. If you have two pads, one to wipe-on and one to wipe-off gently, the results can be quite fantastic. Wipe on thickly, and the colour will smudge thinner and better.

(b) When quite, quite dry (now you know what we meant when we talked about patience), spray with aerosol shellac or varnish.

Scratches and Gouges

These are quite as irritating to deal with as cigarette burns, but no more difficult, because the process is exactly the same.

If the actual wood is damaged, you can treat it with the wax treatment recommended for missing veneers and inlaid pieces. Even if you restore the damaged finish, depressions in the wood will remain, unless you fill them up with something. And wax, in this case, is a quite satisfactory something.

Proceed as for cigarette burns.

Black Spots and Rings

These marks look as if they have been made with black ink that has penetrated through the surface, and into the wood beneath. They are actually discolourations of the wood by prolonged contact with water, possible from a 'sweating' vase, and are particularly noticeable in light woods, such as oak.

Treat as follows:

(a) Make a solution of oxalic acid crystals by pouring them into a cup of hot water until no more will dissolve. (About three rounded tablespoonfuls.)

(b) Brush this solution over the marks, and they will disappear almost instantly.

(c) Wipe the surface a few times with a clean damp cloth, and the job is finished.

Warning. Oxalic acid can be bought by the pound at paint shops. It won't damage any furniture surface, but it is extremely poisonous, and great care must be taken in its use, and in the storage or disposal of any left over after use.

Hazy or Cloudy Finish

Moisture in the air is, over a period of years, a great despoiler of furniture finishes, causing a loss of colour that varies in degree from the faintest grey 'bloom' to the bleached white that shows up after furniture has been left out in the rain. The whiter the discolouration, the deeper it has penetrated into the layer of finish.

Slight Discolouration

This can be treated by a process known as *Abrasion*, which starts with the scraping-off of the top layer of finish. Ordinary hazing and clouding usually affects only the top 5% of the finish, and we're going to remove this 5% with coarse steel wool. *Not* sandpaper, because, however careful you are, you run the danger of cutting too deeply into the finish, and even into the wood itself. This would land you up with a difficult problem instead of an easy one, because you may well find yourself having to apply an entirely new finish.

ABRASION is carried out as follows:—

(*a*) Clean the surface of any wax or polish that may have accrued over the years, using turps substitute, which is half the price of turps, and just as effective. A quart of it will clean one grand piano, or a dining-room table and four chairs.

(*b*) Use a small rag, an old washrag, for instance, to apply the turps substitute, rubbing the surface well. Wipe off with a clean rag.

(*c*) If any debris remains on the surface, it is bound to be water-soluble, and can be removed with a damp rag. Great alien lumps can be lifted with a wooden spatula.

(*d*) Divide a pad of ooo steel wool, like Gaul, into three parts. Using one piece at a time, rub the surface with long straight strokes that follow the wood grain. You can rub across the grain in corners if you have to, but follow the grain as much as possible for a really good effect. Rub each portion of the surface with from five to eight strokes, and then wet the surface with turps to check your progress. (You won't be able to see how things are coming along until you do this.) If hazy patches are left, rub on with your steel wool wet from the turps, which you replace as it evaporates. The idea is to remove only enough of the top layer of finish to get rid of the haze.

(e) Wipe the surface with a dry rag, and wax with a good brand of wax polish.

Worn and Worn-Through Finishes

If a finish on a piece of furniture becomes worn, and this worn finish has developed haze, the layer is not deep enough to stand treatment by abrasion. In some cases spots and haze may have worked right down to the wood, where the stain may have disappeared, and must be touched up before applying new finish.

In case you think that the only thing you can do is to strip all the finish from the surface, and start from Square One, we have news for you. You can do a pretty adequate patch-up job if you follow our directions. The decision as to whether you are going to completely re-finish or apply First Aid is entirely up to you, and depends very greatly on the value of the furniture concerned. An antique piece should probably be re-finished, but a beat-up old family dining table in constant use will respond magnificently to the tarting-up described below. And it's probably what a professional furniture restorer would use, anyway. This process is known in the trade as:

OVER-COATING

(a) Clean the whole surface with turps substitute and water, as described in section (6).

(b) Any areas bare of stain must be recoloured to match the rest of the wood. Professionals use alcohol stains that come in powder form, and when mixed with alcohol, dry in about thirty seconds flat. But a reasonable substitute is a set of artist's oil colours, which will dry in about an hour, because they are going to be used very thinly, and no oil is going to be used in the mixing. A little experimentation should bring you an exact colour match with the surrounding area.

(c) Apply a coat of shellac or varnish, either by brush (see instructions for Varnishing on page 53) or by aerosol spray. These sprays are one of the modern inventions that really benefit the furniture First Aider, and their cost is offset by the fact that you do not need paint thinners or brushes. And they dry in about ten minutes.

(d) When the overcoat is dry, wipe over the surface lightly with ooo steel wool and wax or polish the surface.

Note. To avoid 'pebbling', or the formation of 'curtains' in your over-coat, always have the surface you are treating in a horizontal position. While the surface of a table is naturally in this position, a chest of drawers presents a different problem. Take out the drawers, and stand them so that their faces are horizontal, and turn upwards each surface of the chest before you start to work on it.

Cracked and Chipped Finishes

Worn and damaged factory (lacquer) finishes can be treated by a method known as *Re-amalgamation*, and, suprisingly enough, are extremely easy to deal with, even if the surface of the finish is crackled to the extent that it looks like a crocodile's hide.

Almost all factory-applied finishes are lacquer finishes. You can buy cellulose thinner in any paint or hardware store, and cellulose thinner will dissolve any lacquer finish instantly. (If you don't believe it, try spilling a drop of nail-varnish remover on a lacquer-finished dressing-table. Nail-varnish remover contains cellulose thinner).

By dipping a brush into a small bowl of cellulose thinner, you can actually dissolve and rebrush any lacquer finish, however cracked, unless it is so badly crumbled that it flakes and falls off as you use it.

Of course, there's a little more to it than that, (there always is!) and the correct way to proceed is as follows:—

RE-AMALGAMATION

(*a*) Work in a dry, heated room, or outside on a warm summer day, as humid air will cause the finish to 'cloud', owing to poor patchy drying. Have the surface to be worked in a horizontal position.

(*b*) Pour a cupful of cellulose thinner into a small bowl, and using a brand-new two-inch paint brush (you don't need a tapered or varnish brush), dip into the thinner, and brush *freely*, but not sloppily, on the surface to be reamalgamated. Wet the surface as quickly as possible, using a little more thinner than is necessary to obtain an ordinary brushing consistency. And when we say 'quickly', we mean the whole surface in about half a minute—literally.

(c) 'Tip-off' by brushing with a series of light smoothing strokes.

(d) When completely dry (in ten minutes to half an hour), rub down with ooo or oooo steel wool to remove any roughness, and then wax or polish.

Re-Amalgamating Shellac Finishes

An antique piece which has never felt the hand of a restorer will have, in nine cases out of ten, a shellac finish, and its re-amalgamation, although basically the same as for a lacquer-finished article, differs only insofar as, instead of using plain cellulose thinner, you substitute methylated spirits, with ten or twenty per cent cellulose thinner added to it. Proceed as for the re-amalgamation of lacquer finishes.

Note. You may consider we've been a bit high-handed in instructing you to use a new brush when re-amalgamating, but it is essential that brushes should be absolutely, perfectly clean. Unfortunately the point on which the inexperienced are most likely to fall down is on the cleaning of brushes. Later in this book, on page 33, we give full directions for the *professional* cleaning of brushes, which takes considerable time and care.

We can't stop you from deciding to use an old brush,

but don't blame us if the results aren't quite what you had in mind.

Instant Re-Finishing

This section of the book may sound like a 'Come back all we said', because this is a method, not only of applying a new finish over an old one, but in some cases, of actually filling in minor cracks and scratches, and dealing with a small amount of hazing and bloom.

It's just about as 'instant' as any process can be, because it actually dries as you're working. And it's easy. So if you have a surface that's not too badly crackled, not too deeply hazed, this is a method you might like to try. It's called 'Padding', and it's done with Padding Lacquer. Now you may not have heard of padding lacquer, and neither have a number of paint-shops, so it is better to buy it direct from Hill, Son and Wallace, Bruton Bridge, Manchester 7, or from Cellon Ltd., Kingston-on-Thames. Or try to pursuade your paint shop to stock it for you.

Instead of using a brush, you work with a pad of cotton cloth (a piece of old cotton sheeting is ideal, or old cotton handkerchiefs), and all you have to remember is that you must keep the pad moving. If you stop, even for an instant, the pad will stick, and leave the mark of the weave on the finish.

When padding, the surfaces do not need to be horizontal. This is the professional method of refinishing, and the only trick you have to learn is to keep the pad in constant motion, so that it won't stick, and to remove it with a slow little flourish which takes it off the surface instantly. Or to run it off the side of the surface. You should be able to learn it in five to ten minutes preferably with a 'dummy run' on a less important piece of furniture.

Learn to work in continuous figures-of-eight, to cover the whole surface, then in long strokes for the main area, and little strokes into the corner. Resurfacing a reasonably sized table should take fifteen minutes—and don't stop for *anything*.

Padding lacquer is applied with a pad or rubber, and the best sort is made as follows:

(a) Take a piece of clean, old, non-fluffy, soft cotton cloth, about the size of a handkerchief. In fact, an old cotton handkerchief is ideal. Not a *new* cotton handkerchief, because new materials usually contain 'dressing'. Not an old soft piece of wool or nylon or silk or winceyette. Plain ordinary cotton, which has never been starched.

(b) Spread it smoothly on the table, making sure that there are no creases, and, above all, no seam, hem or embroidery running across it. Its surface must be plain and flat.

(c) Place a triangular piece of cotton wool or wadding just off-centre of the cloth, and bring up the corners of the cloth in a bunch over the top of the triangle.

(d) Lift the pad by the bunched-up material, and pat the rubbing surface smooth. It should rather resemble a mediaeval shoe, with a flat sole and a pointed toe, which is going to help you enormously when you start to work into the corners.

This is a more or less standard pad or *rubber* for

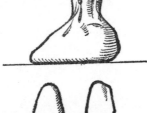

The correct shape
for a 'rubber'.

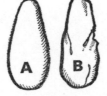

The polishing surface
should be smooth as in A.
Not as in B.

finishing and polishing, and the material to be applied can be poured onto the wadding inside the pad, if the amount to be used has to be controlled. When padding and the lacquer is applied fairly freely, the pad can be dipped into a small bowl containing about half a cup of padding lacquer, and squeezed to remove the excess.

It's a good plan to have several of these pads, because they are very useful, and can be kept, between operations, in air-tight screw-top jars. Professionals believe that you never get your very best results from a new pad, that it must be 'worked in' a bit for the best effect.

Never use a pad for more than one preparation, i.e., your padding lacquer pad must only be used for padding lacquer; and a polishing pad only for polish *of the same colour*. Never use a pad that has become hard and dry, or dusty, or you will spoil the surface you are working on. After all, they're expendable. They take 30 seconds to make, and cost nothing.

PADDING

Proceed as follows:

(a) Pour half a cup of lacquer into a small bowl, dip your pad into it, and squeeze it tight. Later you can wet your pad from a five-ounce bottle, because that is just about the amount needed for an average sized dining table top.

(b) Start stroking the surface in your figure-of-eight movement, dipping your pad into the lacquer as you build up a good coating on the surface.

(c) Start with a gentle touch to wet the surface, and gradually increase the pressure until you are rubbing really hard, to force the hardening fluid into crevices. Cover the main area with figure-eights, and with long strokes across the surface, (working the way of the grain) and with little strokes into the corners, using the 'toe' of your pad. Apply gradually, and remove the pad gradually but cleanly.

(d) When you have been rubbing for about fifteen minutes, and the whole surface is clear and smooth, stop wetting the pad with lacquer, but keep rubbing to complete the drying process, for about four or five minutes more.

(e) You will now have a splendid mirror finish, which will dry overnight, and can be wax polished. If you prefer a 'dull-glow' finish, rub-down the surface with ooo or oooo steel wool, and it will be ready for the next step in half an hour. Divide your steel wool pad into three pieces, and stroke the surface with long strokes following the grain. When the surface is evenly dulled, apply wax polish.

Important Note

If your pad should stick, in spite of all your care, do what the professionals do—apply half a teaspoon of mineral oil to the spot, and then grind smooth with emery paper wrapped round a piece of wood. Wipe with a dry rag.

CHAPTER 2

How to Cut Costs

A number of do-it-yourself enthusiasts will embark on a project just for the pleasure of doing a job, and of getting a professional result, and it is for these home therapeutists that a great number of the present expensive preparations are marketed. If you are in the 'money-no-object' class, then, obviously, this chapter will have no interest for you. But for the average individual, there are several ways in which the cost of furniture refinishing can be cut down, and very often the preparations and chemicals we recommend are exactly the same as the ones that come in fancy shaped bottles and cans under a fancy trade name, and at a very exalted price.

We have already discussed the use of turps substitute in the interests of economy, and of cellulose thinner and/or methylated spirits instead of paint and varnish removers. Now we are going to let you into a few more trade secrets. There are three chemicals commonly used by professional furniture refinishers, and they are caustic soda, ammonia and trisodium phosphate. All cheap, all readily obtainable.

Caustic Soda

Bought at any paint store, and many supermarkets (don't buy washing soda by mistake), caustic soda will work when everything else fails, even possibly some of the high-priced paint removers. It will strip off eight layers of old paint with ease, at the cost of a few shillings, where you might well have to use two gallons of expensive paint remover.

It will also strip off your skin at no extra charge. It is *not* sissy to wear protective gloves when using caustic soda.

Another disadvantage to using caustic soda is that it will only work at 70° F. or over, and this means a warm sunny day. You are going to work outside, unless you have a heated barn or warm cellar with a built-in drain, or dirt floor, because you are going to use a garden hose. It won't do your grass a scrap of good, either.

You will need:

(*a*)   A tin or enamelled pail.

(*b*)   A pair of heavy cloth-lined rubber gloves.

(*c*)   Two cans of caustic soda crystals (for a dining-room table or equivalent, with about eight layers of paint on it), which are commonly sold for cleaning drains. Under trade names, like I.C.I. Lycon, it works just as well.

(*d*)   An old dish mop or a piece of rag tied to a stick.

(*e*)   Plenty of rags.

(*f*)   Vinegar.

MIXING A SOLUTION OF CAUSTIC SODA

The correct solution is a can of caustic to a quart of water. Weaker solutions may be ineffective. The caustic solution may darken the wood a little, but this can be bleached out later with any liquid laundry bleach, such as Brobat, although this darkened wood is often very attractive, and you may decide to leave it unbleached.

Important—always put the water in the pail first, and sprinkle the crystals on top. Reverse the procedure, and the solution will boil up, spatter, and generally make rather a dangerous mess.

Proceed as follows:

(*a*) Dip your mop or rag in the solution and apply it to the paint. As the paint dissolves, add more solution until you are down to bare wood. Use a wire brush or paint scraper to get the paint out of the cracks.

(*b*) Wash the dissolved paint off with water, preferably from a garden hose, or from a 'bucket brigade' of helpers.

(*c*) Wipe the wood dry with rags, and then brush it over with vinegar to neutralize any traces of the caustic. Unneutralized caustic will stop the wood from drying.

(*d*) Rinse the whole piece off, and wipe dry with rags.

Note. Caustic soda is sometimes called 'lye', and you may come across it under that name in old-fashioned books.

Ammonia

Ammonia is used to remove the original base-coat of paint on an antique, which is usually milk paint and rock-hard and although there doesn't seem to be a paint remover in the world that bothers it in the least, ammonia will cut right through it immediately.

(a) Apply the ammonia straight from the bottle with a mop or old brush, or pad of rough steel wool.

(b) Swirl it round until the paint dissolves into a thin paste, rinse off and allow to dry.

Pine and poplar and most fruit woods will darken with ammonia to a pleasing antique brown, but cherry, mahogany and oak may darken a little too much for the average taste. Use household bleach to lighten.

Trisodium Phosphate (T.S.P.)

T.S.P. can be bought from companies who sell soaps and detergents to laundries, because it is an active ingredient of both soaps and detergents. These companies can usually be found in sizeable towns, and if you're lucky, your laundry manager will tell you whom to contact. T.S.P. usually costs about a shilling or two a pound. (See what we mean by cutting costs?)

Although it works very effectively, it is much safer to handle than caustic soda. You are still advised to wear gloves, but it does not burn on contact as caustic soda does, and if you wash away spots of it on your hands within a few seconds, you are fairly safe.

Make a saturated solution with a gallon of hot water, which will take about three cupfuls. Use in exactly the same way as caustic soda, but no neutralizer is needed, and T.S.P. does not darken the wood as caustic is apt to do. Any slight darkening can be bleached out with laundry bleach.

The Proper Way to Clean Brushes

Obviously, to buy new brushes every time to apply lacquer, stain or varnish would be a very expensive business indeed, and since we are out to cut costs, we give you *the absolutely correct method* for cleaning brushes. Using an imperfectly cleaned brush is the best way to ruin a surface, and there is nothing to do about a ruined surface but to start all over again. There are ways in which you can cut corners, but this is not one of them.

Professionals clean their brushes in this way. They are expert corner-cutters, but they don't cut corners here.

(a) Wipe the brush, and squeeze it out.
(b) Rinse in *four* changes of cellulose thinner, using half a cup of thinner every time.
(c) Wash in soap and water four or five times, working up to a lather each time, and rinsing well.
(d) *Start cleaning within five minutes of using the brush*, no matter what it has been used for.
Or buy a new brush.

CHAPTER 3

Refinishing Antique Furniture

In the previous chapter we have dealt mainly with furniture that is 'modern' to the extent that it hasn't come into the antique class yet. Well, actually, everything we have discussed so far holds good for any sort of furniture, except for one very important fact, that when we renovate modern furniture the object is to make it look as new as possible, but when renovating an antique, we have to take care not to spoil the individual character of the finish, and the soft patina that only age can give, while cleaning the wood, and emphasising the wood grain.

Stripping Old Finishes

Let's suppose you've found an interesting potential heirloom in Aunt Emma's attic, or in a junk shop, or on a rubbish dump. It looks terrible, but it seems sound, even though the finish is just about non-existent. You have time to spare, and you'd like to have a go!

You will need:

Rags.   A soup bowl.
An old nylon brush
At least three pads of grade 1 or 0 steel wool,
    which is quite coarse enough (Never use sand-
    paper. Even the finer grades are too coarse.)
A package of ooo steel wool.
A quart of cellulose thinner.
A quart of methylated spirits.

You *don't* need paint thinner as you are using cellulose thinner and meths, which are far cheaper, quite as effective, and remove old paint and varnish faster, because you don't have to wash off any residue as you do with paint thinner.

You can apply a new finish as soon as the old one is removed, and if you use such 'instant' finishing techniques as Overcoating and Padding, you can re-finish such pieces as desks and large tables within two or three hours.

This is because meths and thinners are not only removers but solvents, and dissolve dirty old finishes so that they can simply be wiped away. And since they are volatile, they evaporate completely in half a minute.

You are going to use plenty of solvent, so it is a good idea to stand the legs of the piece of furniture you are working on, one at a time, in the bowl of solvent. This will allow you to slosh around more freely without making an unholy mess of the carpet. Spread news-papers too.

Work in a room with the windows open, even in winter, to let the fumes out. This process is rather hard on the hands. If you still think that wearing gloves is sissy—remember that we warned you!

This is what you are going to do:

(a) Pour about a quarter of a cup of first one solvent and then the other onto the surface to be treated, to see which works better. (Usually they both work equally well). Sometimes they work best mixed together. You'll just have to try them.

(b) Fill your bowl with whichever solvent or mixture of solvents you find most successful, and, holding the bowl near the table, slop on the solvent with a pad of coarse steel wool. Coat the whole top, and keep on slopping until the whole thing is a dirty gooey mess, soaking up as much of the mess as you can by using your steel like a sponge, squeezing it out into an old can.

(c) Finish up by wiping the surface with rags dipped in solvent. A brush can be used on carved legs. Tip the piece of furniture up when doing the ends. It is always easier to work on horizontal surfaces when you're doing a messy job.

(d) Bonus! When you've given a last wipe down, you're not only ready to apply a new finish— you have a base finish already applied, because the remains of the old one is left, in the pores of the wood. So you only need *one* coat of new finish, whereas if you had used paint or varnish remover, you would need two! All this—and money-saving, too!

(e) To apply a quick and most attractive finish, spray with clear, quick-drying spray, let it dry, and wipe down with fine steel wool. Apply a coat of boiled linseed oil, leave for a few minutes, and then rub off *hard* with soft clean rags. This gives the superb dull glow so prized on antiques, but if you prefer a higher shine, the piece can be waxed over the new finish.

Renovating Veneer and Inlaid Furniture

Inlays and veneers are rather fun to repair, and knowledge is extremely useful. Damaged antique pieces of this type are often to be had quite cheaply, because of the time involved in restoration.

Lifted Veneers

In the days when veneering and inlaying were in fashion, glue was made from fish, hooves and hides, and were water-soluble. Waterproof glues are a modern invention. The old-fashioned glues, being water-soluble, became dampened from atmospheric moisture, and from accidental spillage, seeped out, and lifted the veneer or inlay. Dirt, dust and polish collected in the crevices.

The very composition of these old glues makes the task of the restorer much easier. Since they also soften with heat, if the area under the lifted veneer or inlay is perfectly clean, you can often simply iron them down. Cover the affected area with a couple of sheets of waxpaper, add about ten sheets of newspaper, and place your iron, at low heat, on top of that. After ten minutes, take the iron off, and replace it with a stack of books while the glue dries and hardens.

If someone has tried to effect a repair by squirting

glue under the lifted veneer or inlay, take an absolutely new single-edge razor blade, cut off the loose veneer and scrape off the dirt and excess glue from the underside of it, and from the wood underneath. Glue the veneer back into position with any white glue, place under an iron as described above and weigh down with books.

Whether you are simply softening old glue, or removing the old glue and substituting a more modern variety, remove any waxed paper that may have stuck on by rubbing the area gently with ooo or oooo grade steel wool. Cover the whole area with varnish to prevent further lifting, and to seal out the moisture that caused the original trouble.

A word of caution—if you decide to re-lay the whole of a piece of inlay, replace the components one at a time, unless you're exceptionally good at Jigsaw puzzles, or don't mind creating a new pattern which could possibly only be described as—unusual.

Chipped Veneers and Missing Inlays

The easiest way to repair chipped veneers and replace missing inlays involves nothing more complicated than a box of children's wax crayons.

If none of the colours match the missing piece exactly, mix the waxes by melting small quantities in a tablespoon over the kitchen stove. Don't heat them over matches or candles, as you may get soot into the wax-and spoil the colour. Sometimes (but not very often), you can buy special sticks of coloured wax designed for this purpose, which do not need melting, and are simply mashed into the empty space you want to fill.

In either case, the gap should be carefully scraped clean first with your new single-sided razor blade. Melted wax is poured into the gap, and left to harden, when it is scraped flush with a dull table-knife blade.

Since wax offers small resistance to scratching and other damage, it is better to apply a thin coat of shellac, after which you can add varnish if you want a good water—and alcohol—resistant surface.

Refinishing Painted Furniture

It is often possible to buy a decent antique piece that has suffered seven or eight layers of paint since it first saw the light of day. One must remember that no article of newly-made furniture ever had an original value beyond its actual purchase price, and if people liked their furniture painted clean and bright, they did just that, without any thought for their future value as antiques. We might do well to consider this before we smarm paint all over decent modern pieces, which might bring our descendants a better price if we left them alone.

However—we want to remove the layers and layers of paint, and to refinish our antique piece. This can be done with Caustic Soda or T.S.P., as we explain in our Chapter on 'How to Cut Costs'.

Now as you reach the last layer of paint, it is quite possible that you will find yourself with a rock-hard paint layer, which looks ready to defy any chemical known to man. Actually we have explained how it can be removed with nothing more difficult than ammonia.

But before you set to work to remove this milk-paint, stop and think. Milk-paint has a value all of its own, and an article of furniture with a good milk-paint finish is worth twice as much as the same piece with a clear finish. So the removal of milk-paint may well halve the value of your antique.

Milk-paint finishes are usually a dull red, sometimes slate-blue, and, polished, look most attractive. But, as we said before, if remove it you must, ammonia will do it, and the instructions are given on page 32.

Beaumontage

Beaumontage is used in a process known in the trade as 'stopping', when defects in wood are too big to be repaired with ordinary fillers. It is extremely useful when wood has worked apart of the joins, or a knot has fallen out and left a hole, or some other gross damage has occurred.

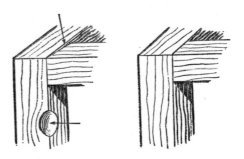

Two cases for Beaumontage,
before and after use

To make Beaumontage:

(a) Melt beeswax and resin in equal quantities, and

add a small quantity of shellac and suitable colouring matter.

(b) Melt the lot in a small can on a warm stove—preferrably not over an open flame, because the mixture is very inflammable.

(c) Keep in a tin, and use as required, in the same way as you use a stick of sealing wax. Carefully smoothed down, it should not show in the least, if your colour match is good.

CHAPTER 4

Finishing Raw Wood

Faced with an unfinished piece of furniture, there are a great number of finishes that you can apply to it, and the choice is entirely up to you. You can leave the wood its original colour, or you can stain it. And having stained it, yo u can seal it with shellac or lacquer, and then have your surface glossy and shiny, or dulled off.

Or you can French polish it, and this is no more complicated than any of the renovation processes we have described in this book. There's a whole chapter later in the book, to tell you how to do it.

Preparing Wood Surfaces

Obviously, before raw wood can be finished properly, by any method at all, the surface must be prepared to make it as smooth as possible.

This is particularly important when the final finish is to be of high polish, whether of French polish or of any other kind, because, while paint will cover up roughness, polish of any kind will magnify it. A little care taken in preparation will avoid the disappointment of a poor final result.

1. Run over the surfaces lightly with a wood scraper held at an angle of about 45° to the surface, paring off fine shavings here and there, until the surface appears smooth.

2. Rub over with No. o glass paper, *always working the way of the grain*.

A scraper, showing the angle and direction in which it should be worked.

Finishing Plywood Furniture

There is a trick to staining plywood, as many a do-it-yourself enthusiast has found out to his sorrow. But the trick is simple—give it a coat of thinned-down shellac, (half shellac and half meths), before staining. It's as simple as that. The shellac sinks into the soft areas, and ensures that the stain goes on evenly.

Here's how it can be done:

(a) Give a coat of a solution of half shellac and half methylated spirits.

(b) When dry, rub down the whole surface with ooo grade steel wool to smooth the surface, and remove some of the shellac from the hard streaks in the grain.

(c) Apply stain.

A FAR, FAR BETTER WAY

This is a nudge in the direction of the gentle art of furniture-faking, quite legitimate unless you are going to sell the piece as being of better wood than it actually is. Apply two coats of shellac, rubbing down each coat with steel wool when dry. *Wipe on* a pigmented oil stain, and you can make even plywood look like any wood you choose. For a darker stain, stand your stain for a while, then pour off the clear top liquid before stirring.

Later, when we come to Staining in detail, we take the lid off this business of 'faking' woods, and show you how to stain practically any wood to resemble another, more expensive one.

Finishing Pine Wood Furniture

Quite the best way of finishing pine furniture is to use a one-coat, wipe-on sealer finish. Now it's quite possible that the paint-shop man will tell you that he doesn't have any furniture sealer, only floor sealer. Well, you'll have news for him—they're exactly the same thing. If he doesn't have the colour you want, squeeze a tube of oil colour into a pint of clear sealer.

These tubes of colour are exactly the same as those used for tinting paints, and you will want what are called 'earth colours'—raw and burnt sienna and raw and burnt umber. Mix them until you get the colour you want, but *beware of red*. It's a tricky colour where wood is concerned, and almost always turns out to be too red on the finished product.

Proceed as follows:

(*a*) Apply the coloured sealer by brushing it on freely, or mop it on, or put it on with a rag. Apply until it stops sinking into the wood, and some traces remain on the surface for ten minutes after the application of the last coat.

(*b*) Wipe off excess with rags or paper towels, and let the wood dry overnight.

(*c*) Rub down with ooo steel wool to smooth the surface, and wax with a good wax polish.

This is a very easy process, and will give you perfect results every time. And, equally important, you will have as serviceable a finish as you can find anywhere in the world.

How to Make and Apply Stains

If you have a good piece of wood of good colour, it is often better to leave it unstained but this is, of course, quite an individual matter, and when the wood is not as attractive as you might like, staining is the usual answer. (There are others, such as the fuming of oak, which we deal with in due course.)

Although they are easy to apply, there are a great number of different stains, and various ways in which they can be made, and a little clarification might not be out of order.

The three basic types of stain are:

(a) Water stains
(b) Spirit stains, not to be confused with the bottled stain-and-glaze mixture often sold under this name.
(c) Oil stains.

WATER STAINS are easier to apply than spirit stains, because they dry more slowly, and therefore can be laid on more evenly, but you need more coats to get depth of tone. This is actually an advantage, because a slow build-up of colour is much more effective. But, of course, the whole process takes longer.

But almost everything in life has its disadvantages, and, of course, water stain is no exception. The wetting of the wood causes the grain to swell, and creates an uneven surface, which must be rubbed with glass paper, *when the surface is dry*, to avoid 'fluffing'. This occasionally creates bare patches, where the stain has been rubbed off, and more stain must be applied.

SPIRIT STAINS dry in a few minutes after the last coat has been applied. Brush the way of the grain, and carry the brush right to the end of the wood, or you'll get darker patches where you over-brush, and if you brush the whole section again, you'll get a darker strip. And if you paint right over the surface again you may have a darker colour than you intended.

OIL STAINS dry slowly, and are therefore easier to control. The oil soaks deeply into the wood, and gives it a mellow appearance. But you have to wait for two or three days after staining and before polishing, which some people find a disadvantage.

How to Improve Woods

1. **TO IMPROVE MAHOGANY**
   (a) To make mahogany richer in appearance, use a solution of potassium bichromate in water.
   (b) To darken mahogany, dissolve the bichromate in liquid ammonia.
   Keep your hands out of any potassium bichromate solution, and expose the wood to sunlight before you judge its full depth of tone.

2. **TO IMPROVE WALNUT**
   Oiling will enrich the appearance of walnut, two or three light applications being more effective than one heavy one. If there are light patches, stain them with powdered Vandyke Brown in water or spirit.

3. **TO IMPROVE SATIN WALNUT**
   Satin walnut can be enriched by staining with yellow ochre, and polishing with a colourless polish.

4. **TO IMPROVE ROSEWOOD**
   Boil a quarter of a pound of logwood chips in a pint of water, and stain the rosewood with the solution, used hot.

5.　TO IMPROVE OAK

(a) *Darkening* oak is effected by sponging the surface with liquid ammonia, repeating until you obtain the desired effect.

(b) *Fuming* oak is probably the best way to darkenen oak, but it's rather tedious, and needs a certain amount of care. Once again, ammonia is used, but it is the fumes that do the work. (Hence the name). And you'll need a large, virtually air-tight cupboard.

1. Place the article to be fumed in an *empty* cupboard and put one or two trays or saucers of strong ammonia on the floor.

2. Seal the cupboard, and we really do mean *seal*. If ammonia escapes, not only will the wood not darken, but people in the house may suffer the unpleasant effects. Put cellotape over the cracks between the door and the lintels, or stuff them with newspaper. Leave for at least twelve hours.

3. If dark enough, coat with clear polish, using a brush, and finish as required.

Note: Small articles are better put into a large box, instead of a cupboard, If results of fuming are patchy, cover the dark parts with clear polish and re-fume.

If your piece of furniture has folding or shutting parts, unfold and open. That is to say, open doors and drawers.

The Gentle Art of Wood-Faking

There are any number of ways in which a cheap wood can be made to look like a more expensive one, and don't think it isn't done, every day of the week, in the furniture trade.

Here are some of the ways:

MAHOGANY FINISH

(a) Stir a small quantity of powdered Bismark Brown into methylated spirits, adding an ounce of orange shellac to every tumblerful of spirit. Use with caution, as Bismark Brown is a very powerful stain.

(b) Should the above stain be too fiery in colour, use an ounce of red sander's wood in a tumblerful of methylated spirits. Or add a touch of spirit black.

(c) Or add powdered Venetian Red to linseed oil, and put in a small quantity of liquid driers.

(d) A cheap way to achieve a mahogany finish—mix equal quantities of stale beer and water, adding a tablespoon of powdered sienna for each pint of solution.

(e) A Chippendale mahogany finish—tint wood with a walnut stain, and polish with a red polish.

(f) A Sheraton mahogany finish—stain as in (a) then use red oil, made as follows:
Steep two ounces alkanet root in half a pint of raw linseed oil for at least a day.
Finish by polishing with red polish.

WALNUT FINISH

(a) Mix equal quantities of powdered burnt umber and Vandyke brown in a little liquid ammonia, and dilute with water according to the depth of stain required.

(b) Or take ten parts powdered Vandyke brown, one part American potash, one of nut galls. Put the nut galls in forty parts of water, and then add the two other ingredients.

(c) Or put a teaspoonful of permanganate of potash in a pint of hot water; also put a tablespoon of Epsom salts in a pint of hot water. When both have dissolved, stir them together, and use warm.

(d) Or make strong coffee, strain it, and add Vandyke brown as required.

(e) Brunswick black, made into a flowing liquid with turpentine, makes a useful, but not particularly high-grade, walnut stain.

SATIN WALNUT FINISH

Take raw sienna, mix with a small quantity of burnt sienna, mix with a little flake-white, (not mixed with oil,) and stir the mixture into water. Add a little chrome yellow if you like.

Go over the surface with a cloth when nearly dry.

ROSEWOOD FINISH

Stir a small quantity of powdered Venetian red into linseed oil, and add a very little drop black.

OAK FINISH

(a) Take a teaspoonful each of potassium bichromate and powdered burnt umber, stirred into a pint of hot water. Use hot, and then wipe away surface moisture with a cloth.

(b) Or take a teaspoonful of permanganate of potash and about half the quantity of powdered burnt umber, stirred in a pint of water.

(c) Or apply a solution of a tablespoon of potassium bichromate in a pint of boiling water. When dry, put on a coat of drop black, thinned to a treacly liquid with turps. Lightly wipe the surface as soon as this is applied, leaving the black in the grain. Paint on a coat of French polish, (see page 66) and treat with a wax polish. Rub down with glass paper or coarse steel wool between each application.

(d) Or put two ounces of asphaltum in a tumbler of turpentine, and give one or two coats, as required.

EBONY FINISH

Real ebony is seldom met with, because it is expensive, and difficult to work with. Close-grained woods such as sycamore, holly, cherry and apple make good ebony-substitutes, as does mahogany. Ebony stains can be made as follows:

(a) Fixed Indian ink, sold by artist's colourmen. Give two or three coats.

(b) Or boil an ounce of logwood chips in a pint of water until one third has evaporated. Use hot, and follow with a solution of half an ounce of sulphate of iron in a pint of hot water.

(c) For a more intense black, add an equal quantity
of nut galls to logwood chips in solution (b).

SILVER-GREY FINISH

Woods can be bleached to a silver-grey finish by
applying two or three coats of a solution of one
part silver nitrate in fifty parts water, then cover
the surfaces with weak spirits of salts, and, when
this is thoroughly dry, paint with a solution of
one part ammonia, ten parts water. Put the
article away in a cupboard for a day or two,
and then use a wax or oil polish. Do not French
polish.

Note: No matter how good your colour-eye, always
try stains on odd pieces of wood before actual use on
furniture.

Faking Wood Grain

Where grain is a feature of the wood, as in walnut and
rosewood, colour-faking is not enough. You're going to
have to add the grain.

You're going to need a steady hand and some degree
of artistic ability to accomplish this well—and if it can't
be done well, it is better left alone. To be a successful
wood-faker you also have to know the various grains,
or at least have a piece of authentic wood from which to
copy.

Grain is applied with a feather, and there are two
methods, one of which entails the direct application of
a very dark stain, and the other, the application of a
chemical that causes the basic stain to darken.

(*a*)   1*st method*. Take some French polish (see page 66) and mix it with some powdered black. Apply with a feather to simulate the desired wood-grain, after staining has been finished, and before oiling.

Graining wood with the tip of a feather.

(*b*)   2*nd method*. Apply as above, using half an ounce of sulphate of iron, dissolved in a pint of water.

Use the tip of the feather, and have a rag handy to smear out a faulty line, or tone down one that is too prominent.

Varnishing

Nearly everybody has trouble with varnishing, usually with billions of tiny bubbles. But varnish is one of the most useful finishes that one can apply, because it doesn't re-act either to water or alcohol, and is therefore ideal for table tops. It's non-sticky, and doesn't obscure the grain of the wood. It's relatively quick to apply, and comparatively inexpensive.

Because of all these advantages, varnish can be forgiven for being a bit difficult to apply. And if you follow these instructions, you really shouldn't find it difficult at all.

(a) Buy a brand-new can of either furniture or floor varnish—they're both the same. Don't, what ever you do, use spar varnish, even if you have a can left over from the last time you serviced the yacht! Spar varnish always remains slightly tacky, the better to resist temperature changes. If you don't believe us, try it, but always have someone else within call, to help prise you loose from your table top. And don't use left-over varnish—buy a new pint for every job.

(b) Buy a brand-new two-inch paint brush. This is no moment for economy, even if you have washed your old brush according to our instructions. Once you have used your new brush, never, never use it again for varnishing.

Yes, we did say a *paint* brush. No, we did not make a mistake. Varnish brushes are for experienced tradesmen; in an inexperienced hand, they produce millions of bubbles. And the proper use of varnish brushes isn't learnt in five minutes. Or, possibly, in five years.

(c) Buy a brand-new pint can or bottle of paint thinners or turps substitute. Not, under any circumstances, pure gum turpentine, which impairs good drying.

(*d*) Prepare the wood surface, and stain it according to our instructions.

(*e*) Pour a cup of varnish and a quarter cup of paint thinner into a small bowl. The mixture may be on the thin side, but don't worry. This is how it should be.

(*f*) Brush on helter-skelter, every which way, until the whole surface is covered.

(*g*) Brush smooth with the tip of the brush, with long strokes that go from edge to edge.

(*h*) Go away and leave it to dry by itself. If you must come back and peep, *don't try to do anything about the brush marks*. They'll smooth themselves out.

(*i*) The next day, scuff the surface with ooo steel wool, using light strokes from edge to edge, following the wood grain.

(*j*) Apply a thin coat of paste wax and polish with a soft cloth.

(*k*) Spill a martini on it, if you feel inclined!

Wax Polishing

At various intervals in this book, we've talked about wax polishing, and now we've come to the stage of dealing with it in greater detail.

Wax polishing does not give as high a shine as French polishing, and many people prefer it for this very reason. Wax polishing emphasises wood grain, and is therefore particularly suitable for coarse-grained woods, such as oak, and, to a lesser degree, mahogany.

There are a great number of proprietary wax polishes on the market, but wax polish is easy to make, and it is extremely important that all ingredients should be pure and of good quality, and, let's face it, often the only way to make sure of this nowadays, is to make it yourself.

Wax polishing is the usual alternative to varnishing after wood has been stained, and all the stains we describe earlier are suitable for wax polishing *unless they have a water base*. If you intend to wax polish, substitute turpentine for water when making these stains.

Melting Beeswax in hot water is the only
recommended method.

Making Wax Polishes

(*a*) Shred half a pound of pure bees wax and melt it in a pint of turpentine. Do this in a tin can, and stand the can in a bowl of boiling water, making sure that the can stands steady, and doesn't float and overturn. Beeswax and turpentine is a very inflammable mixture, so it's better to use the hot water method than to try to heat the mixture over a flame. Change the water as it cools down, and it will be ready in about half an hour.

(b) And that's all—except that you should keep the polish in a tin, and never let it stand with the lid off, as the turps will evaporate. You can add appropriate colour to your various polishes if you like. You can even incorporate the stain you wish to use in them, but even if this appears to save a little time, it's a bit tricky, and you'll probably get better results if you stain and polish separately.

Polishing

(a) Thin out your first coat of polish with a little turps, which will help it to sink into the wood. Rub in all directions, with the grain and against it, using a rag. You get better results if the room is warm enough to warm the wood slightly.

(b) Wait at least an hour. (Sorry, wax polishing *cannot* be hurried). Then apply a stiffer (undiluted) coat of polish with a rag, and work it in vigorously with a stiff brush, such as a small shoe brush. (Keep your brush specifically for this purpose, and don't use it for anything else).

(c) Work as much of the wax as possible into the wood, leaving the thinnest possible film on the surface, so that it will harden quicker. A thick film will take *months* to harden, and will remain tacky, and smear and bruise at every touch until it has hardened properly.

(*d*) To get the best effect, use a small quantity of wax four or five times in a fortnight, giving each layer a chance to harden. Or wax occasionally for *months*. Your final surface, if you have followed these instructions, should be rock-hard-with a depth of lustre that no short-cut method could ever give you.

Warnings

(*a*) Don't try to get a high glaze, because you won't. There are ways of getting a high-glaze finish, but this isn't one of them.

(*b*) Always have your surfaces bone-dry. The wax won't 'take' on a damp surface.

(*c*) In cold weather, work in a warm room, and warm the wax slightly.

Wax polishing is by far the best gloss finish for antique furniture, because, let's face it, the piece has probably been wax polished from its infancy. French polish, a comparatively modern invention, and the easily applied high glazes, usually look out of place, especially as the original wood was probably selected with an eye to its appearance *when wax polished*.

Oil Polishing

Oil polishing is another tradition treatment, often found in antique furniture. Oil polished furniture shows a dull sheen that many people find very attractive indeed.

There are no tricks in oil polishing, and no short cuts, either. Simply rub the surfaces over very sparingly with linseed oil on a soft rag, and rub vigorously, every day for about a fortnight. You can, if you like, use a stiff brush kept solely for the purpose, for all but the last two or three applications. Use a soft woollen rag for these.

CHAPTER 5

French Polishing

We've saved French polishing until last, like the icing on the Christmas cake, because a great number of enthusiasts consider it to be something of a crowning achievement in a lifetime of furniture refinishing, like Everest to a mountain climber.

Many people have the idea that French polishing is so difficult that it really is a job for the expert—and a very expensive expert at that. Well, if you've read this book, and had a dab at a few of the processes in it, you'll find that we have, with low and calculated cunning, brought you up to a stage where *almost every process involved in French polishing* is already familiar to you.

And if you've cheated a bit, (which you're quite entitled to do—after all, you bought the book), and turned straight to this chapter, you can simply turn back and look up each process as you come to it.

Nothing in this book has been difficult, and nothing in this chapter is going to be difficult, either. You'll be surprised!

This is what you are going to do:

1. Prepare the surface of the wood (page 42)
2. Stain the wood. (page 45)
3. Oil the wood.
4. Fill in the grain.
5. Polish.

And we're going to explain the last three processes as we come to them. But before we do, there is something special to say about staining.

Staining During Polishing

However well you may stain an article of furniture, it's usually made of several pieces of wood, which may vary very slightly in hardness, and may absorb the stain to different degrees. This applies even when all the pieces of wood are of the same type.

These variations in the resultant stain-tone may not be very noticeable, but polishing emphasises them. However, you'll be glad to hear that the matter is easy to deal with.

(a) Take some polish as described on page 57 and dilute it with twice the quantity of methylated spirits—an egg-cup full should be enough.

(b) Take another egg-cup, and stretch a piece of muslin across the mouth of it. Put a little heap of the appropriate powdered colouring on the muslin.

(c) Pour the diluted polish through the muslin, so that some colouring will be carried with it. If the resulting mixture is not dark enough, repour through more colouring until you find it satisfactory.

Staining the polish
Pour some of the ordinary polish on to a muslin strainer
which already carries some colouring.

(d) Take a small soft brush, and stand it in spirit for a few minutes, until the hairs soften.

(e) Paint the liquid over the lighter areas of wood with the brush going the way of the grain. Allow to dry completely before going over a second time, but drying is rapid.

(f) When dry, run over the painted areas with coarse steel wool, and wipe with a dry rag.

(g) Coat with transparent polish, and leave for twenty-four hours before continuing with the next stage.

Oiling

The piece of furniture to be French polished is oiled before polish is applied, and this is done after the prepared surface has been stained, and the stain is absolutely, perfectly dry. Or, if you stain and polish in one operation, oil before this. Oil emphasises the wood grain, enriches and mellows the appearance of the wood.

(a) Apply raw linseed oil with a soft non-fluffy rag, or rubber, coating all surfaces evenly and lightly, including corners and angles.

(b) Look at the wood from all angles to see if any patches have been missed, and if so, re-oil them. When oiling mahogany, use red oil, made by adding one ounce of alkenet root to a pint of oil for a light finish, more for a darker one.

Warning

The wood does not need a *bath* of oil, just a light, even, coat. Over-oiling will cause the wood to 'sweat' after the polish is applied, and may crack the surface of the finish.

Filling the Wood Grain

All wood surfaces are pitted and porous, the extent varying according to the type of wood. Close-grained woods, (maple or sycamore) are very slightly pitted, while open-grained woods such as oak are far more porous.

Obviously, in all woods, if left untreated, the polish will sink into pores and cavities, and the final surface will be uneven. So we use fillers, spread them over the surface, (against the grain) and wipe them off, so that the filler only remains in the pores and cavities, and the surface is event

We have a choice of fillers, and they can be bought in dry form. But they can also be made at home, as follows:

(a)   Sift plaster of paris, coloured to the appropriate shade with powdered colouring, into a little heap. Sprinkle methylated spirits onto a cloth pad, and dab it into the pile, rubbing it over the wood.

Warning

Do not mix all the plaster and the meths before applying to the wood, as it sets very quickly, and you will get an instant and very free-form sculpture.

Do not substitute water for meths, although it might appear to work just as well, because it will cause the wood grain to swell, and more unevenness will result.

(b)   Or take equal parts of dry whitening and plaster of Paris, add the appropriate colouring, and mix with enough turps to make a very wet paste. Add a few drops of gold-size, and use rapidly.

(c)   Or paint the surfaces with the following varnish:
3 ounces orange shellac
½ ounce powdered resin
½ pint methylated spirits
Use two or three coats, according to the porosity of the wood, allowing each coat to dry thoroughly before applying the next, and going over the surfaces each time with very fine glass-paper or coarse steel wool.

Stopping

Stopping is used where there are defects too large to be treated with filler, particularly where two pieces of wood do not fit exactly. Use Beaumontage, which we have already dealt with on page 40.

Polishing

Well, now we really come to the heart of the matter, to the processes that separate French polishing from any other kind of finishing. Again—nothing difficult, because basically all furniture finishing processes are the same. Only the ingredients vary from time to time.

1.   Have plenty of rubbers handy, made as we described on page 25. And remember, even if these rubbers can be stored in air-tight jars, and used again, keep each rubber for its own particular function, which is only plain common-sense.

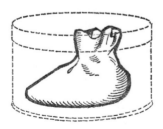

If it is not used within about 10 minutes, always place the 'rubber' in a sealed tin or jar.

2.   The liquid which produces the shine in French polishing consists of two main ingedients, shellac

to give body and substance, and a spirit to dissolve it in, and make it workable. Since this is all there is to it, there is absolutely no need to haul off and buy expensive made-up polishes at the paint store. You'll probably get far better results if you make up your own, because you'll know that you're using first class ingredients.

3. Dissolve five ounces of orange shellac in a pint of methylated spirits, and add a teaspoon each of gum arabic and gum copal. The latter two ingredients are not absolutely necessary, but they do give better results. Leave the whole lot overnight, (or at least for half a day) before using.

Warning

Check that your methylated spirit does not contain resin. Methylated spirits is normally and legitimately adulterated with something, (to make it even more undrinkable) and resin is one of these substances.

Stained Polishes

In the case of some specific woods, stains can be included in the polish, and it is as well to be quite sure about these.

Mahogany. Use an ounce of Bismark brown to each pint of polish, or four times the quantity of red sanderswood.

Walnut. Add a few drops, (not more than a teaspoonful) of spirit varnish to each pint of polish.

Ebony. Add aniline black to the polish.

Yellow woods. Substitute button shellac for orange shellac, and colour with gamboge. You'll have to experiment to get the right colour—on a spare piece of the same wood.

Light woods. You're going to need a transparent polish, so make it up by using eight to ten ounces bleached shellac to a pint of meths.

Now we're going to get down to the actual polishing, which consists of three separate operations, namely:

1. Bodying-in

2. Building-up

3. Spiriting-out

All these three operations are going to be carried out in a warm, dry, dust-free room, so it's as well to start yesterday, clean the room thoroughly, give the dust time to settle, and turn the heaters on. Cold and damp will make it difficult to bring the wood surfaces to their proper condition, and the result will be smeary and dull. Dust will, of course, scratch the surfaces if it gets on the rubbers.

And take off knobs, brass handles etc., on the piece to be polished, so that you can work in long sweeps without having to go round obstacles.

1. Bodying-In

You are going to lay a surface of polish over new wood, and the quantity needs to be fairly lavish, so that a 'skin' is formed.

(a) Open out your rubber, and sprinkle polish lavishly onto the inside pad, so that polish oozes out when squeezed. Be quick about it, because the polish dries fairly fast.

(b) Gather up the corners of the rubber, and run the surface of it across the faces of the wood, first across and then against the grain, so that not a pin-head of the surface is missed. Up into the corners, too.

(c) Change to a circular motion, and to figures-of-eight, until the polish in the rubber is exhausted, and the surface begins to shine.

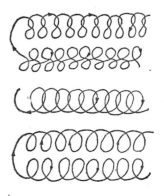

Three alternatively correct methods of moving the 'rubber'.

(d) Now a shine is exactly what you *don't* want at this stage. What you want is 'body'. Recharge your rubber with polish, and go on with your circles and figures-of-eight.

(e) Momentary drying during this process is a good thing, and it's not a bad plan to work on *two* surfaces at once, rubbing them alternately. If your surface is constantly wet, you'll pick up the body you've already laid down, so that you're actually working against yourself. The surface dries quickly, however, and your rest periods need not be very long.

(f) The centre may begin to body-up faster than the corners, and there's a lot to be said for the old adage 'Look after the corners, and the centre will look after itself.'

(g) When a fair amount of polish has been laid evenly over the whole surface, you're going to leave it until next day in your dust-free room, (or a dust-free cupboard, if you have one, and your piece of furniture will fit in it). And see that it stays dust-free. Seal up the room, if you must, in the same way as you sealed the cupboard when fuming oak. Just don't let anyone in, especially if there's a breeze blowing.

(h) The following day, when the surface is hard, and has formed a firm base, very little of the polish you are going to apply will sink in. *This is the first and only secret of French polishing.* If you try to cut corners, and omit the first operation, you are not really French polishing at all, and you are not going to end up with a French polished surface.

Before Building-up you prepare the surface as follows:

(a) The surface will not be quite even, because there will be pin-point depressions in it. If you hadn't filled-in, there would be giant craters to deal with, but you've been too wise for that. So you simply run over the surface lightly with steel wool to even out the pin-points.

(*b*)　Apply the polish lightly, first with and then against the grain, and then in circles and figures-of-eight. (Corners! Corners!)

(*c*)　Your rubber is likely to stick a little, because you are not rubbing, (you don't need to. You did all that yesterday), but wiping the polish lightly over the wood. So you're going to be cute and clever, and add a lubricant. Take your rubber, which is charged with polish *inside* it, and apply two or three drops of linseed oil to the *outside* of the polishing surface. Now the rubber will float over the surface, and when it begins to drag, add another two or three drops of oil. No more than two or three, and always to the outside.

Dropping oil on the sole of the 'rubber'.

(d) When the surface has an even depth, (but no shine) stop work for twenty-four hours. Yes, twenty-four. Sorry about that, but its essential, because ...

(e) On returning to your work, examine the surface carefully from all angles, you may find that a few pin-points are back, and you're going to have to body-in again. And each time you find pin-points, (where the polish has sunk into the wood pores), you are going to have to body-in again. Waiting the 24 hours between each operation. Of course, you can usually avoid this by doing your first bodying-in really well, and by remembering that very porous woods can drive a French polisher crazy.

Building-Up

Before you start the process of building-up, which is an actual build-up of polish, you have to make sure that your surface is not only smooth, but level. Now a wood surface is hardly ever absolutely level, and so you resort to a simple little trick to level out any depressions. These depressions should not be confused with the pin-points that give us such trouble in bodying-up, because these are spots in which all the polish has sunk into the wood, and can be seen because they are without polish. The depressions we are talking about are suitably covered with polish, but are little valleys in the wood itself.

We are going to use a pounce-bag, a useful little gadget made from a square of cotton cloth about the size of a female handkerchief, and we're going to put an ounce of fine pumice in the centre of it. Gather up the edges, twist them and tie them with string, and your pounce-bag is made. (Keep it clean in a box or jar when not in use. You'll probably need it again)

A Pounce Bag containing fine pumice powder.

USING A POUNCE-BAG

1. Slap the bag on any depressions you notice on the surface, so that the dust creeps through the rag and fills the depression.
2. Take a rubber charged with spirit, and dab a little oil on the surface of it.
3. Work the rubber very very lightly over the dusted parts.

Warning

Use spirit and not polish, inside the rubber. Polish will collect the pumice dust and turn it into mud.

BUILDING-UP

1. Run over the surfaces with steel wool, and wipe away the dust.

2. Moisten the pad inside your rubber slightly with polish and use two or three drops of linseed oil on the outside surface. You use a lot less polish in building-up than you did in bodying-in, because all you want is a 'skin' on the surface. Your pad will therefore be drier, but care must be taken that it does not become too dry, or it will act as an abrasive on the surface.

Check your rubber in the following ways:

(*a*) If your rubber drags, press it heavily on a piece of clean paper. If the mark shows no oil, re-oil the surface. If it shows no polish, recharge your rubber with a small amount.

(*b*) If you draw your rubber lightly across a bodied-in surface, and it leaves a wet trail, you're using too much polish.

(*c*) If the surface of your rubber looks dry and clean, it needs recharging and re-oiling.

(*d*) If your rubber marks are shiny, you are using too much oil. Your rubber marks should be dull.

Oil adds nothing to your work. It is only there to make it easier, and too much of it will make the surface sweat later. The best way of applying it is off your finger, which has been moistened with oil from the neck of the bottle.

Avoiding Marks

You're now at a critical stage, when marks can spoil your work. If you make a mark, you may have no alternative but to leave the surface to dry, and rub it down with steel wool before building-up again.

Therefore, *don't* pick up the rubber from the centre of the surface, but slide it off the edge.

don't put it down in the centre of the surface, but slide it in from the edge.

don't rub too hard. You've done all the hard rubbing when you were bodying-in. *Stroke* the wood lovingly, moving the rubber in continuous circles and figures-of-eight.

don't hurry. Too much energy causes streaking, and may pick up some of the body underneath. (And then you know what will have to happen!)

don't stop the continual motion of your rubber, or it will stick, and you'll be in real trouble.

Never allow the 'rubber' to stand on a surface that is still being polished.

When you're beginning to feel pleased with the surface, its smoothness and depth, switch to a thinner polish, that is, the normal polish diluted with an equal quantity of methylated spirits. Continue with this.

Continue, in fact, until the surface is smooth and deep, and looks perfect in every respect. Except one. It's smeary.

Spiriting Out

Of course, the last thing you had in mind was a smeary surface, so we're going to have to do something about it. Well, the first thing we do is wait. (If French polishing teaches us anything, it teaches us how to wait. Jumping the gun spoils more French polishing than any amount of dust, damp, cold, and bad handling).

We're going to wait at least five or six hours, or overnight, and then we're going to proceed as follows:

1. Take a fresh rubber, with a double thick outer cover, damp it with a little spirit, and leave it (while our piece of furniture is drying-out), in an air-tight jar or tin, so that the spirit permeates evenly.
2. Wipe the surface with light loving strokes, and the smears will disappear.
3. Take another, dry clean rubber, and burnish the whole surface energetically with circular strokes, finishing off by following the wood grain.

Warning

Spirit actually dissolves a little of the surface of the polish and smoothes it out. If you use too much spirit, you will dissolve too much of the polish. Remember that the polish remains soft for two or three days—treat it with the utmost respect and Tender Loving Care.

Egg Shell Finish

Dull finishes, known in the trade as 'egg-shell finishes', are becoming increasingly popular, and it is quite possible to treat your French-polished piece to give it a beautiful dull mellow finish.

Proceed as before until you reach spiriting-out, because instead of spiriting-out, you're going to take a saucer of pumice powder, and a saucer of linseed oil. Fold a rag into a smooth pad, dip it first in oil, and then in pumice.

Run the rag gently over the polished surface, back and forward along with the grain, *not in a circular motion*.

Stop the instant every particle of shine has been removed, or you'll wear away too much polish.

And that's all. That's all there is to the big bogey of French polishing. You can now re-finish a grand piano or a dining-room table, or any piece of furniture that takes your fancy. And get an expert finish every time.

Finally we include some of those frighteningly simple tips which 'sort out the men from the boys', so to speak.

They come straight from the professionals mouth and can be adapted to fit many of the jobs that you are now able to tackle.

Use them whenever you can. They will save you time, and when you have been able to invent some more ideas of your own you will be well on the way to becoming a professional yourself!

Cut a piece of cork as illustrated and it will provide a pourer for your Polish bottle.

When a small piece of wood has to be polished, anchor it down to another piece of wood if possible.

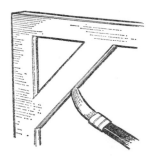

When dealing with fret work, apply plain varnish to the edge *before* polishing.

To polish carved wood, use a brush and a mixture of polish with varnish.

Index